Vocal Selections from

Striking 12

T0052779

A Rewired Version of *The Little Match Girl*
by IIans Christian Anderson

Book, Music, and Lyrics by
BRENDAN MILBURN, RACHEL SHEINKIN,
and **VALERIE VIGODA**

Original cast recording
available on PS Classics

Original New York City production produced by Nancy Nagel Gibbs and Greg Schaffert

Logo designed by Wendy Kenigsberg

Photos by David Allen and Joan Marcus

Purchase of this score does not constitute permission to perform.
Applications for dramatic performances of this work should be addressed to:

Theatrical Rights Worldwide
1359 Broadway, Suite 914
New York, NY 10018
1-866-378-9758

www.TheatricalRights.com

Alfred

Produced by
Alfred Music Publishing Co., Inc.
P.O. Box 10003
Van Nuys, CA 91410-0003
alfred.com

ISBN-10: 0-7390-6629-3
ISBN-13: 978-0-7390-6629-4

Foreword

By late 2001, Valerie Vigoda, Gene Lewin and I had been trying to "make it" with our rock band GrooveLily for eight years. Our dream was to get signed by a major label and play big concerts in front of thousands of screaming fans, but we were starting to hit the rubber ceiling of the music industry. Every time we managed to play a showcase for record executives, they would tell us, "I like this music, but it's too. . . theatrical. It's too Broadway."

We would beat ourselves up trying to shoehorn ourselves into a mold that fit what we thought would play well on radio, and we met with what could be described as limited success: we were playing 150 shows a year and pretty much supporting ourselves with our music. But we were getting tired of the grind, and were seriously questioning how much longer we would want to keep doing this.

November, December, and January were always fallow, dry months for us; gigs were thin on the ground, and we had to scrounge other ways to support ourselves. In 2000 and again in 2001, Valerie took a job as concertmistress of the Trans-Siberian Orchestra, a heavy metal Christmas music spectacular that has become a multi-platinum success and sells out concerts every holiday season.

I went to see Val play with them in San Francisco in 2001 and enjoyed the show immensely—lasers, fog, long-haired guys in tuxedos, and a bombastic version of "Carol of the Bells" is my idea of a good time—but I was struck most by how they threaded the concert with rhymed verse and the hint of a story to hold the evening together. I thought to myself, "We could do something like this!"

Striking 12 was born out of a desire to create a secular holiday show for GrooveLily, a way to keep the band together, happy, and working during the holiday season. Connections at NYU led to a meeting with not-yet-famous playwright/bookwriter Rachel Sheinkin, and Rachel was struck by the poignancy of one of Valerie's songs, "Little Light":

With my coat turned up, my back against the rain

I will cup my hands to shield this fragile flame

There's a bonfire blazing just around the bend

And it would be so easy to toss my match right in

All my friends are there together

Warmth, safety and a soup can

I've been struggling here forever

And everybody's running past me to the dry land

I see all the other torches

Lighting up the night

I am right here with my matches

   burning bright

And no one needs my little light

No one needs my little light

No one needs my little light

Valerie, of course, was writing during a moment of self-doubt, penning a song about trying to make music in a world where it seemed nobody was listening. Rachel heard this song and was immediately reminded of Hans Christian Andersen's *The Little Match Girl*. Rachel found the public domain translation, read all two-and-a-half pages of it, and was astounded at the incredibly depressing ending. . . and from her (and our) reaction to the story came the seeds of *Striking 12*.

Ted Sperling (who would go on to direct *Striking 12* off-Broadway to great acclaim) was in the audience at a showcase of ours in February 2002 at Joe's Pub, and he cornered us afterward, asking if we had any theatre pieces in the works. We mentioned that we were beginning to write a holiday show for GrooveLily, and his response was, "Can you have it finished in time for November so we can put it on in Philadelphia?"

And so we began a race to complete the first version of the show. The songs in this folio were written with Rachel, Val and me on the floor of our subletted Brooklyn apartment; in the practice rooms downstairs at the NYU Graduate Musical Theatre Writing Program in the East Village; and over cell phones with Val and me arguing about lyrics as we drove through the Midwest from gig to gig, while Rachel chimed in over speakerphone from Brooklyn and Gene looked on, bemused, from the back seat.

Somehow we finished a first draft by November of 2002, writing the overture in the van as we drove into Philadelphia. After four days of rehearsal and tech, we got up on stage at the Prince Music Theater and played *Striking 12* for the first time. Our lives have changed completely as a result of this show: GrooveLily is now a band that does (almost exclusively) concerts with a story, happily signed to the theatrical record label PS Classics and playing 25–30 gigs a year. In addition to performing, Val and

I write musicals and songs for animated movies, and Rachel has gone on to win a Tony Award for her book of the musical *The 25th Annual Putnam County Spelling Bee*. *Striking 12* has gone on to be performed all over the country (and in Korea!) by other trios, quartets, and quintets of talented musician/actors, and we've even adapted the piece to be performed by as many as 12 actors and 6 musicians. Judging from the photos and videos we've seen of high school and amateur productions, the piece works really well that way; there's a kind of "let's get everybody together and put on a holiday show in the barn" vibe that fits perfectly with our little story about a guy rediscovering Hans Christian Andersen on a lonely New Year's Eve.

This folio of songs is our Opus 1, the first sheet music we've ever had published. Rachel, Val and I are very proud of these songs and the show they came from, and we're very grateful to you for bringing this music home with you. We humbly suggest that you play hard, sing loud, and throw caution to the wind.

Brendan Milburn
Glendale, CA
October 2009

CONTENTS

Last Day of the Year

Words and Music by
BRENDAN MILBURN, VALERIE VIGODA
and RACHEL SHEINKIN

WOMAN SOLO

What are you gon - na do on New Year's Eve?

What are you gon - na do on New Year's Eve?

THE MAN

I was

late to work   Now I am work-ing late   My

Last Day of the Year - 11 - 1
33475

6

boss said please   I got-ta please the boss   So I

phone the man   I got-ta man the phones   I got-ta

check those facts   I got-ta fax those checks

And I got-ta___ fix that___ print - er   It'-ll be a - no - ther___ late night

Am11

G(add9)/B

I will get— through this— win - ter   With-out a   ray— of   day-light

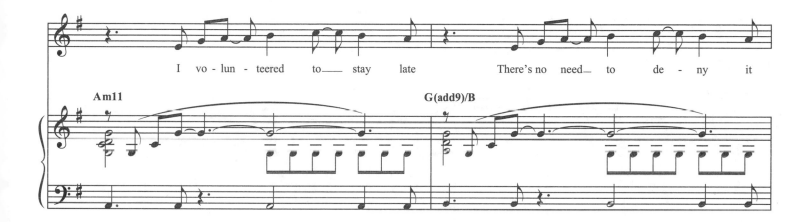

I   vo - lun - teered   to— stay   late   There's no need— to   de - ny   it

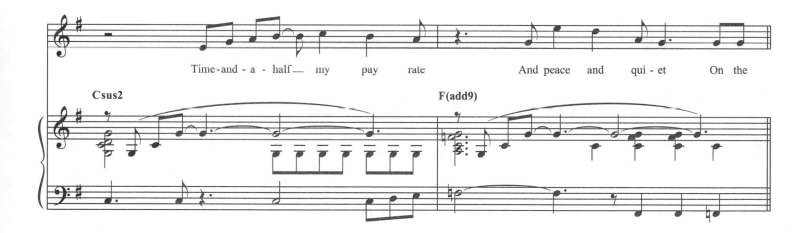

Time-and - a - half— my   pay   rate   And peace   and   qui - et   On the

last— day— of— the   year   The

last_____ day____ of____ the____ year

WOMAN SOLO

What are you gon - na__ do__ on New Year's__ Eve?_____

G(add9)   E♭+/G   Dm7/G   E♭+/G

THE MAN

What are you gon - na__ do__ on New Year's__ Eve?_____ I'm

G(add9)   E♭+/G   Dm7/G   E♭+/G

al - most done____ Now I have done it all_____ I am the

détaché

mp

last one out I'm out at last I go

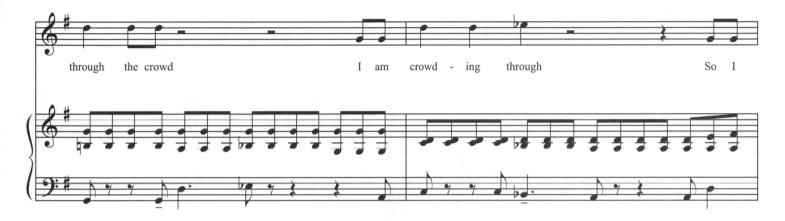

through the crowd I am crowd - ing through So I

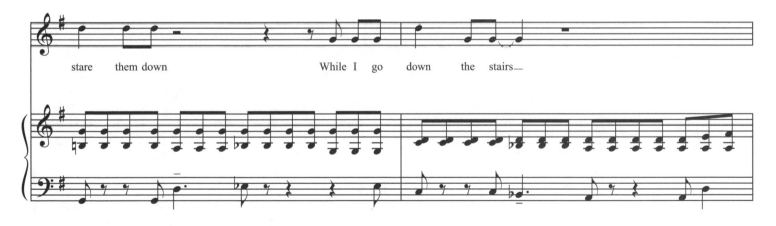

stare them down While I go down the stairs—

CHORUS
lightly

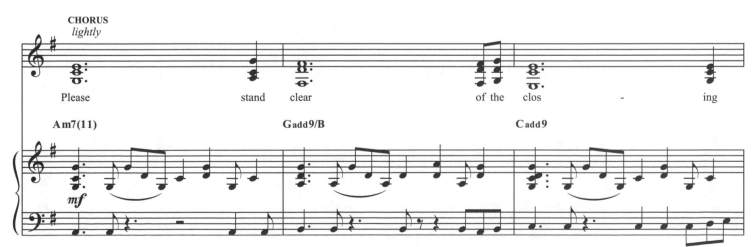

Please stand clear of the clos - ing

Am7(11) Gadd9/B Cadd9

Last Day of the Year - 11 - 6
33475

I ne-ver read those top ten books——— Ne-ver took that trip to France———

——— Did noth-ing to——— im-prove my looks——— I ne-ver learned to sal-sa dance———

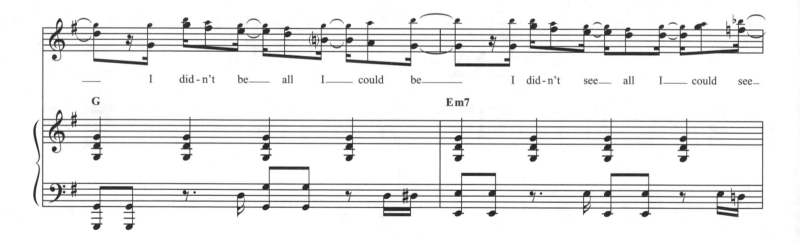

——— I did-n't be——— all I——— could be——— I did-n't see——— all I——— could see———

——— I did-n't call——— on Mo-ther's Day——— I can-not wash my sins a-way———

And I would not dwell on the past If time would not go by so fast

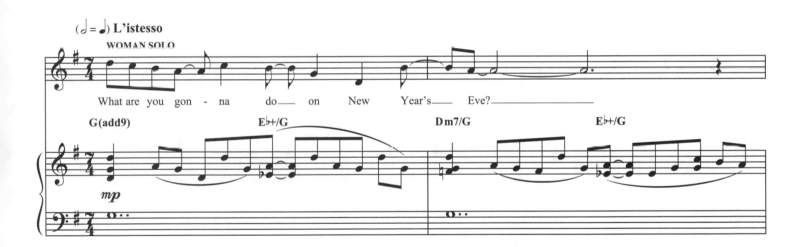

I can't be-lieve al-rea-dy it's the last day..... of the year

$(\rho = \rho)$ L'istesso

WOMAN SOLO

What are you gon-na do on New Year's Eve?

THE MAN

What are you gon-na do on New Year's Eve? I'll

Snow Song
(It's Coming Down)

Words and Music by
BRENDAN MILBURN, VALERIE VIGODA
and RACHEL SHEINKIN

Quiescently, like the first snowfall ($\bullet = 76$)

S.A.D. LIGHT SELLER

Snow - flakes   fall   like   vel - vet_____   from

i - ron_____   co - lored   skies_____

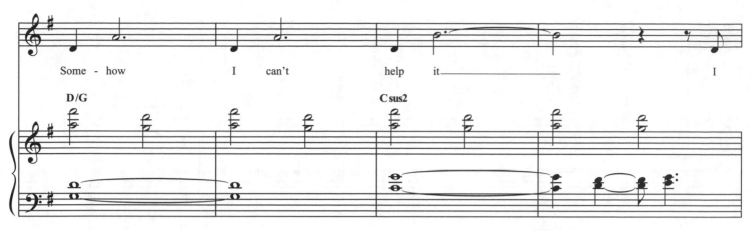

Some - how I can't help it _____ I

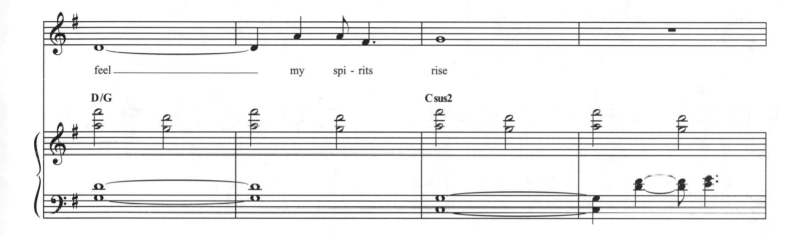

feel _____ my spi - rits rise

Street - lamps a - glow ____

time to take it slow ____ it's com-ing

down

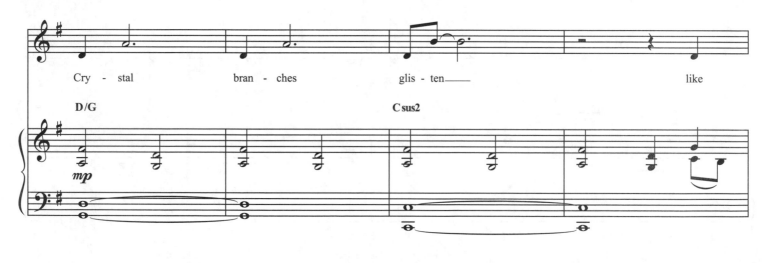

Cry - stal bran - ches glis - ten_____ like

dia - monds_____ o - ver me

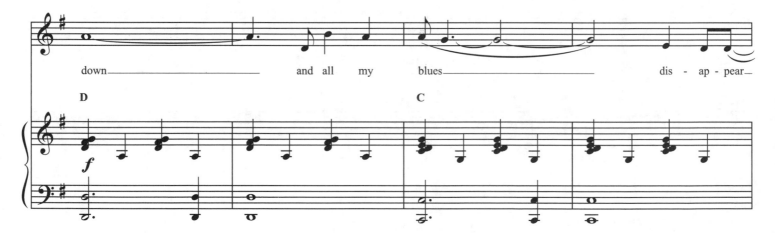

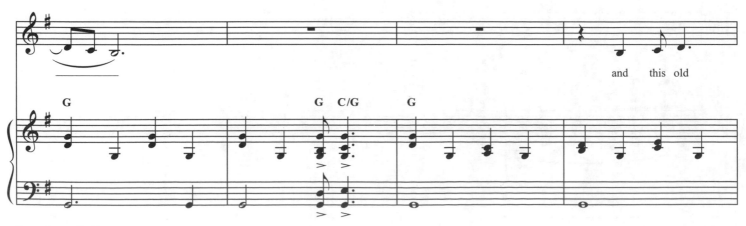

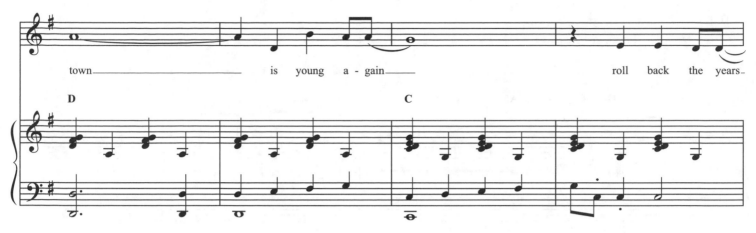

town_____ is young a - gain____ roll back the years__

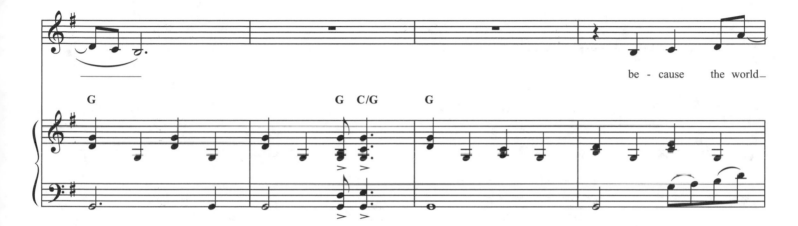

be - cause the world__

looks like new____ or at least__

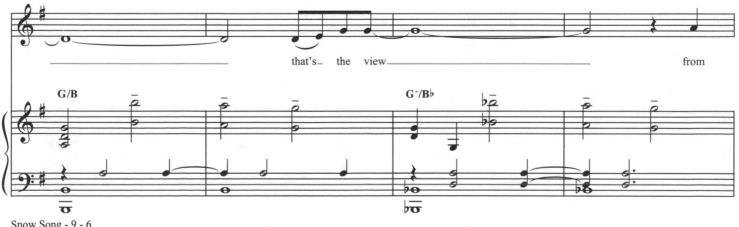

that's__ the view_____ from

Snow Song - 9 - 6
33475

here _____ from _

A7   G6   A7   G   A7   G6   A7

here _____ It's

A7(♭5)/C

cold   here   by   the   ri - ver   but

D/G   Csus2

mp

I _____ don't feel it _____ much   the

D/G   Csus2

Lyrics:
moon's a sil - ver sli - ver

close e - nough____ to touch

storm - clouds drift a - way____

a star comes out____ to play and it's com-ing

Chords: D/G, Csus2, Em9

Open, soaring

down_____ it's com-ing

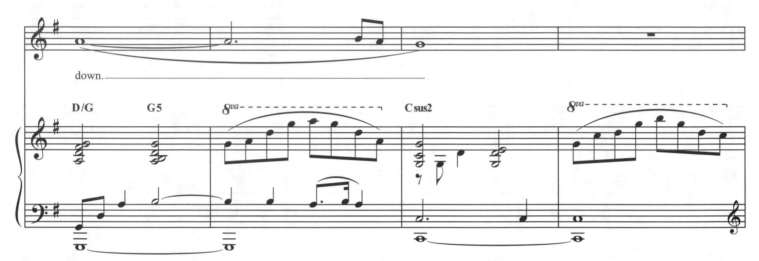

down._____

molto rall.

Resolution

Words and Music by
BRENDAN MILBURN, VALERIE VIGODA
and RACHEL SHEINKIN

Easy groove, swing 8's (♩ = 140)

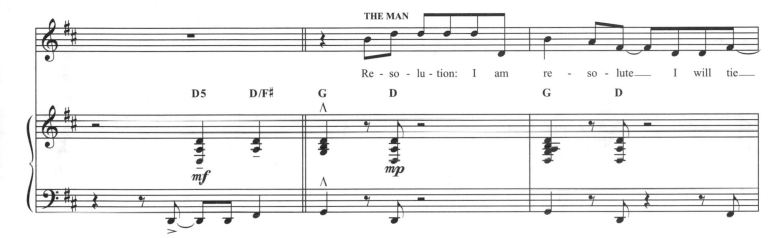

THE MAN

Re - so - lu - tion: I am re - so - lute___ I will tie___

___ no tie___ I will suit___ no suit   I won't be go - ing out

on the town___ 'Cause my   angst   is   up___ and my   bat - te - ry's run   down

Resolution - 5 - 1
33475

Half-time groove

What's there to ce - le - brate a - bout?

I'd ra - ther stay at home and grout

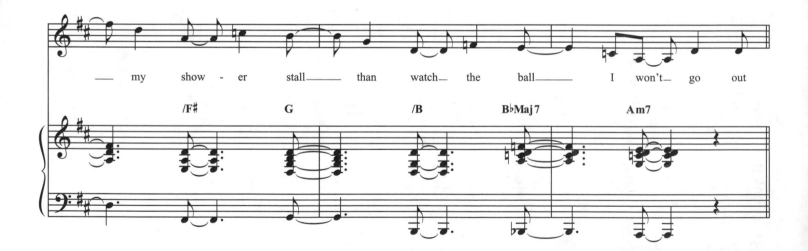

— my show - er stall____ than watch____ the ball____ I won't go out

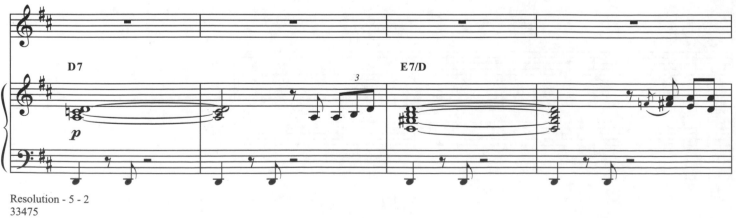

Half-time groove

Who needs to see my so - called friends? —

G   A   G/B   A/C♯   D   D7/F♯

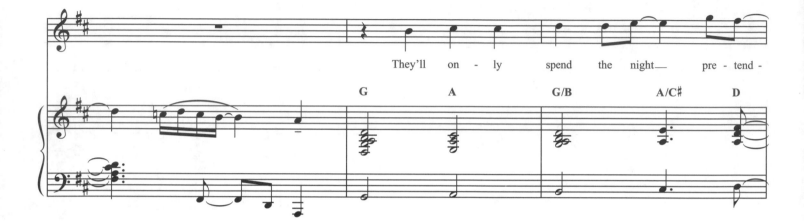

They'll on - ly spend the night — pre - tend -

G   A   G/B   A/C♯   D

ing there's — a way —— on New — Year's Day —— to start —— a - gain.

/F♯   G   /B   B♭Maj7   Am7

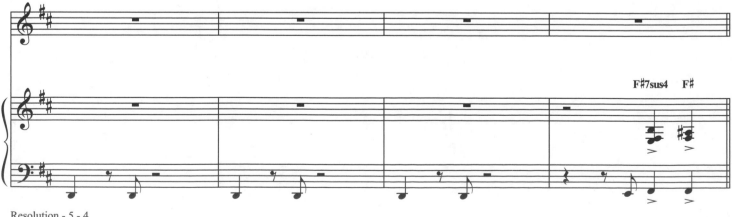

F♯7sus4 F♯

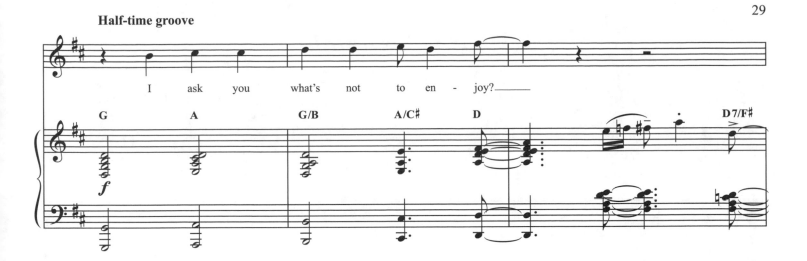

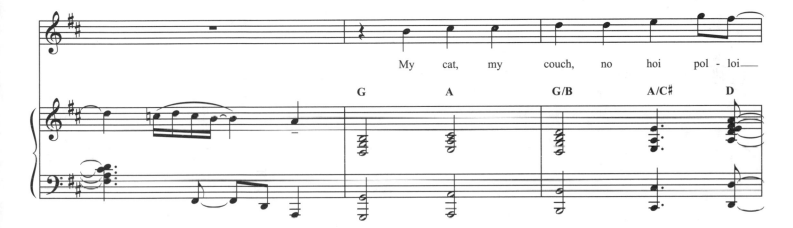

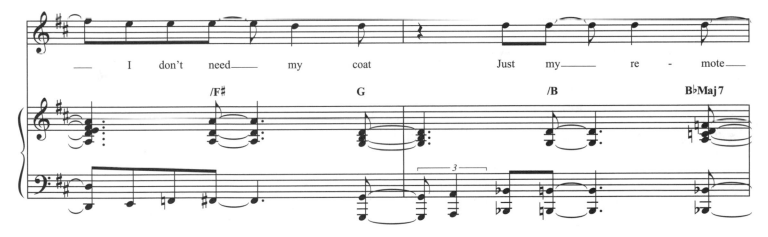

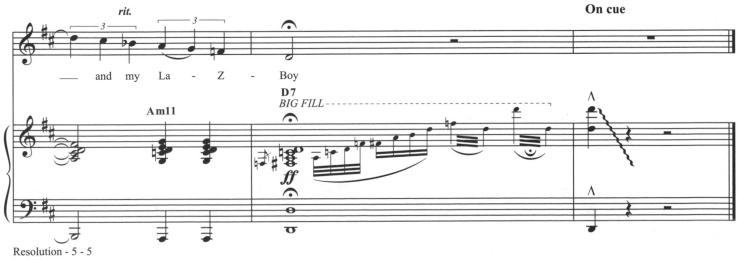

Resolution - 5 - 5
33475

The Sales Pitch

Words and Music by
BRENDAN MILBURN, VALERIE VIGODA
and RACHEL SHEINKIN

pla - ces where you ne - ver think to scrape a broom   For have you no - ticed you have

trou - ble get - ting mo - ti - va - ted?   And have you felt that get - ting   out of bed is o - ver - ra - ted?

And peo - ple who have SAD can   gain   a   lot of weight in win - ter   With the ma - ny car - bo - hy - drates

they con - sume   So now be - fore you go and   lose a - no - ther win - ter to the

THE MAN: *I'm sorry. That was 63 and 1/2 seconds.*
S.A.D. LIGHT SELLER: *No, you're kidding. Can I try again? I swear I
can do it faster. It would just be one more minute out of your life. Please?*
THE MAN: *Well... Sure, okay.* S.A.D. LIGHT SELLER: *1, 2, 3, 4 [MUSIC]*

The Sales Pitch - 11 - 4
33475

With the ma-ny car-bo-hy-drates they con-sume

So now be-fore you go and

— and the year— went by— so fast

Oh, look she's still

Bb7sus4   Bb7   Ebsus4   Ab   Eb/Ab

lose a-no-ther win-ter to the blues you ought-a buy a string of lights or two *Your place is love-ly*

talk - ing   I should pay at - ten - tion

Ab7   Db/Ab   Dbm/Ab   Ab   Bb//Ab   Bbm//Ab

but it's kind-a dim and you could use a lit-tle light to pe-ne-trate the gloom

I don't real-ly think I need— a-ny lights

Ab/C   A°7/Cb   Bb7   Eb7sus4   Ab

THE MAN: *Great. That was 57 seconds on the button, I'm sure that's gonna sell you a whole bunch of light bulbs.*

Underscore

S.A.D. LIGHT SELLER: *I hope so! It hasn't been going too great so far. The last place I went to, they slammed the door in my face and said,*
"Get lost, little light bulb girl!"
THE MAN: *Oh, I get it, it's a literary reference, right? Like "The Little Match Girl." It's kinda nice…*

S.A.D. LIGHT SELLER:
Nice? Do you know what happens in that story? [EXIT SAFETY]

THE MAN

Let's see the Lit - tle Match Girl what did hap - pen in that sto - ry was it Bro - thers Grimm or may - be

S.A.D. LIGHT SELLER

Nei - ther one——

THE MAN

Doc - tor Seuss? No, that's not right the lit - tle girl is sel - ling match - es in the

The Sales Pitch - 11 - 9
33475

40

Green and Red

Words and Music by
BRENDAN MILBURN, VALERIE VIGODA
and RACHEL SHEINKIN

Piano solo

(sample solo, ad lib. as desired)

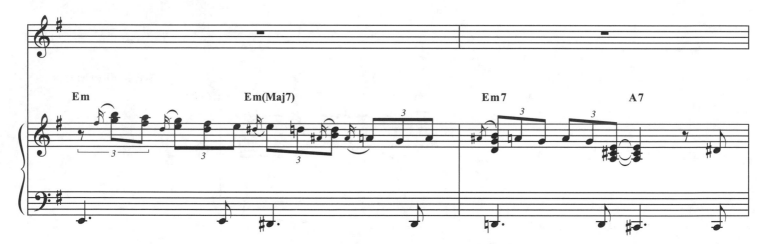

Green and Red - 6 - 4
33475

46

Green and Red - 6 - 6
33475

Wonderful

Words and Music by
BRENDAN MILBURN, VALERIE VIGODA
and RACHEL SHEINKIN

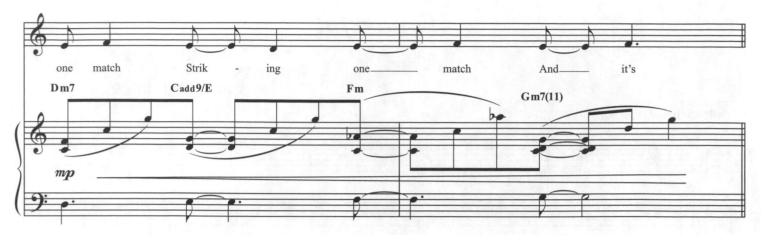

one match   Strik - ing   one___ match   And___   it's

Dm7   **Cadd9/E**   **Fm**   **Gm7(11)**

mp

Won - der - ful___   Warm - ing up my fro - zen fin - gers

C   **G/C**   **F/C**

mf

Won - der - ful___   Like a can - dle bright - ly burn - ing but more

C   **G/C**   **C7sus4**

Won - der - ful___   I can feel   the ice   melt a - way___

Dm7   **Cadd9/E**   **Fm6**   **Gm7**

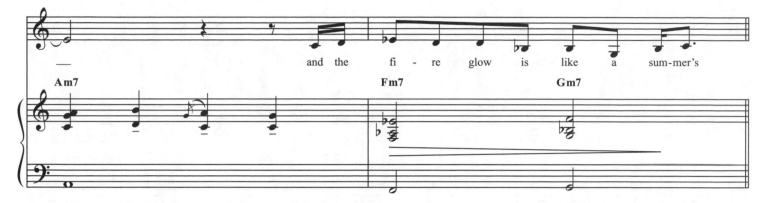

and the fi - re glow is like a sum-mer's

Am7   Fm7   Gm7

NARRATOR 1: *"And it seemed to the girl that she was sitting by a large iron stove. How the fire burned. It seemed so beautifully warm that the child stretched out her feet as if to warm them, when lo! The flame of the match went out, the stove vanished, and she held only the remains of the half-burnt match in her hand." [EXIT SAFETY]*

2x   *Safety*   1.2....   Last time

day

LITTLE MATCH GIRL

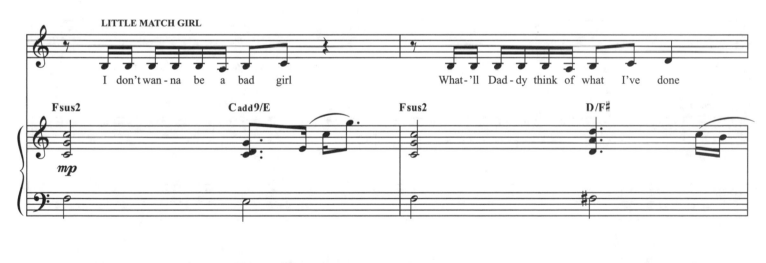

I don't wan-na be a bad girl   What-'ll Dad - dy think of what I've done

Fsus2   Cadd9/E   Fsus2   D/F#

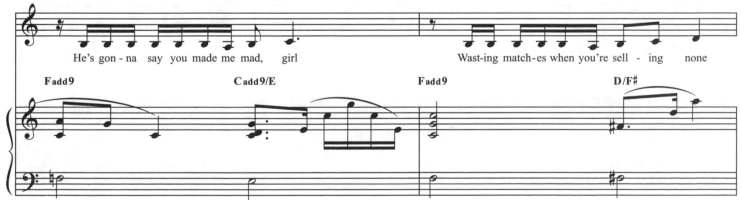

He's gon - na say you made me mad, girl   Wast-ing match-es when you're sell - ing none

Fadd9   Cadd9/E   Fadd9   D/F#

Won - der - ful _____ All the sil - ver po - lished to a

glow And the ta - ble cloth as clean and white as

NARRATOR 1: *"Then the match went out and the feast too vanished. Before her remained nothing but the thick, damp, cold wall."*

[Underscore]

snow

With more drive

LITTLE MATCH GIRL

All of the things ___ I see ___ through win - dows _____

THE MAN

All of the things ___ I see ___ through win - dows _____

When I'm on the wrong side of the glass

When I'm on the wrong side of the glass

C(no3)/G   Am7   Fsus2

Are ev-en more beau-ti-ful and won-drous

Are ev-en more beau-ti-ful and won-drous

C(no3)/G   Am7   Fsus2

Here in the light of just one match   Let the

Here in the light of just one match

C(no3)/G   Am7   Fsus2

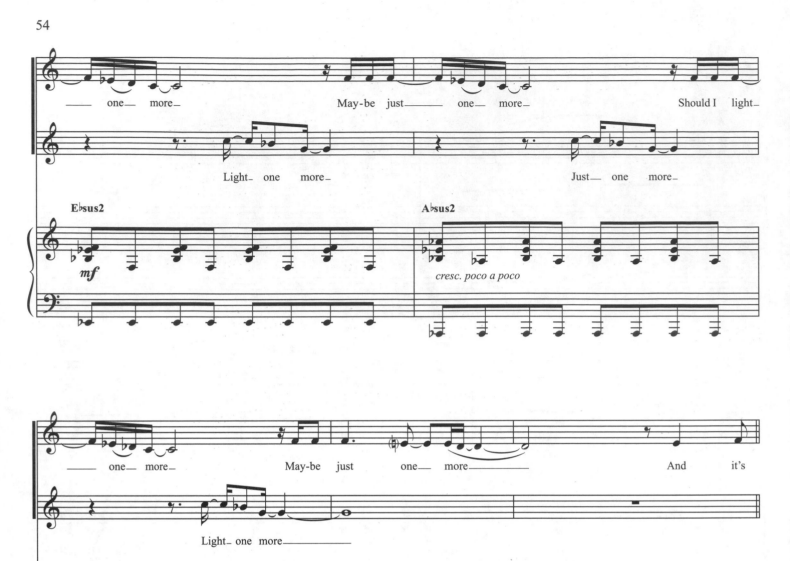

one more___ May-be just___ one___ more___ Should I light___

Light___ one more___ Just___ one___ more___

Eb sus2 Ab sus2

mf *cresc. poco a poco*

___ one___ more___ May-be just one___ more___ And it's

Light___ one more___

Db sus2 G sus4

Won - - - der - ful___ I am here be - neath a Christ-mas tree___ so

C *poco ad lib.* G/C F/C

sub. ***mp***

Won - der - ful___ All the ta - pers shine like dia - monds but more

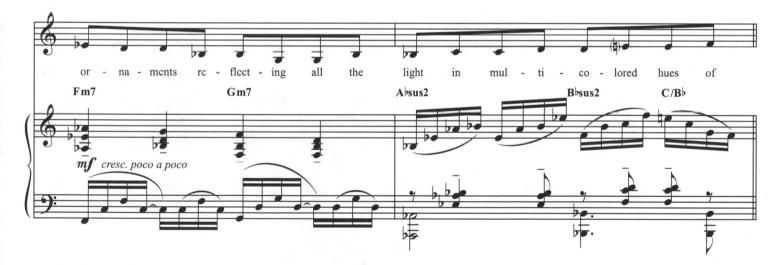

Won - der - ful___ How the branch - es spark - le in the night___ With the

or - na - ments re - flect - ing all the light in mul - ti - co - lored hues of

Won - der - ful___ Like a thou - sand thou - sand con - stel - la - tions

Won - der - ful___ Like a sea of can - dles ris - ing toward the

skies   Can't be - lieve_ my eyes___

Can't be - lieve_ my eyes___   Can't be - lieve_ my eyes___

Caution to the Wind

Words and Music by
BRENDAN MILBURN, VALERIE VIGODA
and RACHEL SHEINKIN

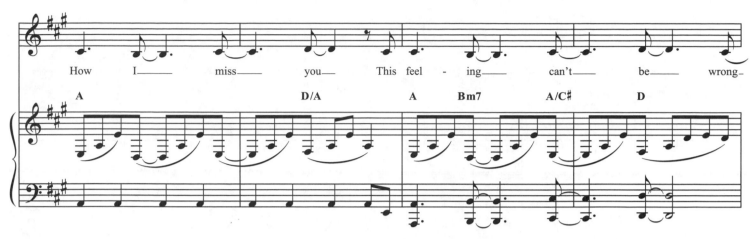

How I miss you This feel - ing can't be wrong

Half-time feel

You told me "Ne - ver hold back a - ny - thing

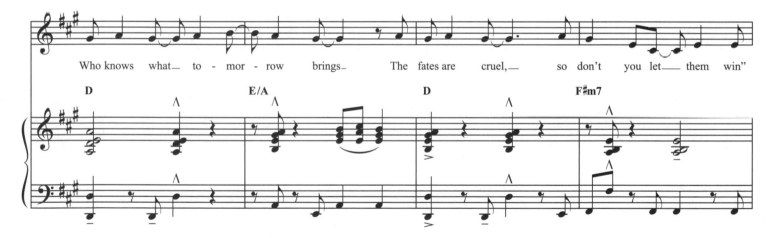

Who knows what to - mor - row brings The fates are cruel, so don't you let them win"

Oh no You lived your life just like a flame That

burned out fast,— but seared— your name— A - cross my heart— and ev - ery - where— you'd been

D   E/A   D   F#m9

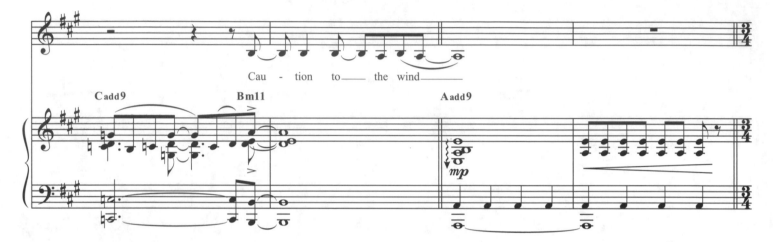

Cau - tion to— the wind—

Cadd9   Bm11   Aadd9

Subito - misterioso

I   will   be   with   you a - gain   Sure   as

Fsus2   Csus2   Dsus2   Fsus2

I   have   ev - er   been   Burn   my   match - es

Csus2   D   Em7   D/F#   Fsus2   Csus2

to the end_____ Throw - ing cau - tion to the wind_____

NARRATOR 1: *"And she made haste to light the whole bundle of matches for she wished to keep her grandmother there."*

SMALL PART GUY: *"And the matches glowed with a light that was brighter than the noon day, and her grandmother had never happeared so bright or so beautiful."* *[EXIT SAFETY]*

Underscore
Vamp   *Safety*

With intensity, building
LITTLE MATCH GIRL

Get - ting_____ clos - er_____ Take me_____ with_____ you_____ I

A   Bm7/A   A   D/A   A   Bm7/A   A   D/A

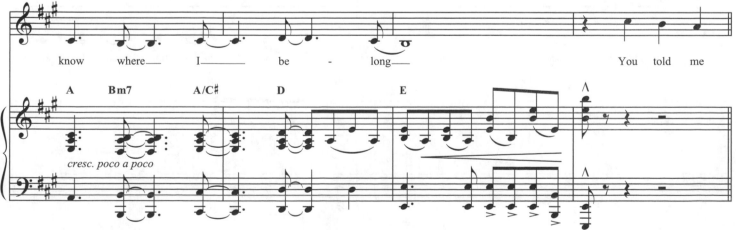

know where_____ I be - long_____ You told me

A   Bm7   A/C#   D   E

cresc. poco a poco

Ad lib. — full out to end

Screwed-Up People Make Great Art

Words and Music by
BRENDAN MILBURN, VALERIE VIGODA
and RACHEL SHEINKIN

Funky latin ($\quarternote$ = 136)

Latin groove

JACK: *All right, listen. Let me tell you something about Hans Christian Andersen.*

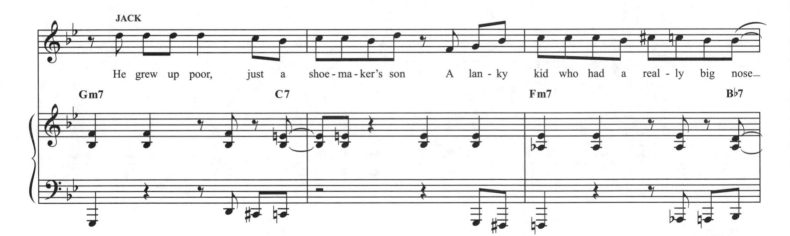

JACK

He grew up poor, just a shoe-ma-ker's son A lan-ky kid who had a real-ly big nose

In - se - cure, im - ma - ture, he was of - ten found

Screwed-Up People Make Great Art - 16 - 1
33475

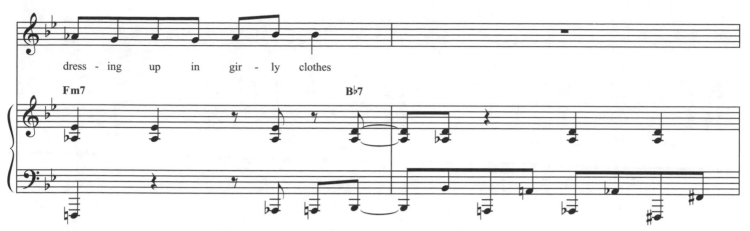

dress - ing up in gir - ly clothes

Fm7   B♭7

His fath - er died and his mo - ther ex-plained that the Ice Mai - den took him a - way

Gm7   C7   Fm7   B♭7

That lit - tle lie made him cry, gave him night-mares and it

Gm7   C7

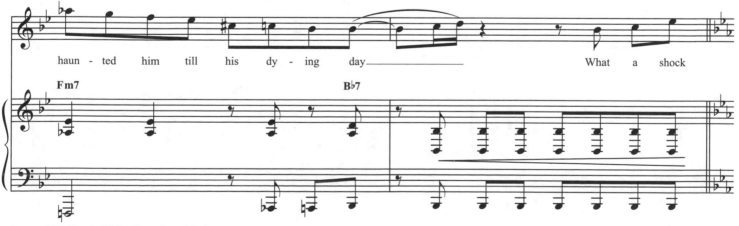

haun - ted him till his dy - ing day____ What a shock

Fm7   B♭7

Rock groove

Yeah it wound—

— him up in-side just like— a cuck-oo clock

_go - ing tick_____ tick tock_____ ('cause)

Latin groove

Screwed-up peo - ple make great art

They shoot right from the screwed-up heart—

Screwed-up peo-ple bare their souls—

Gm7   Eb7

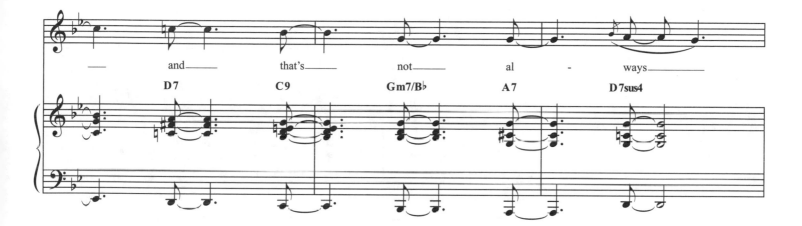

— and— that's— not— al - ways—

D7   C9   Gm7/Bb   A7   D7sus4

smart

Gm7   C7   Fm7   Bb7

JACK

Now our man Hans had a heart full of love— but his fee-lings were-n't al - ways re - turned—

Gm7   C9   Fm7   Bb9

Screwed-Up People Make Great Art - 16 - 4
33475

Rock groove

CHORUS WOMEN

Ooh

CHORUS MEN

Ooh

JACK

So he wrote

wor - ried he'd be bu - ried a - live _____ So in - sane

pain

pain

_____ a lot of fai - ry tales _____ to ease the pain

Latin groove

Screwed - up peo - ple send us post-

Screwed - up peo - ple send us post-

Screwed - up peo - ple send us post-

Gm7

E♭7

cards____ from____ a____ world____ a - part

cards____ from____ a____ world____ a - part

cards____ from____ a____ world____ a - part

D 7   **C 9**   **Gm7/B♭**   **A 7**   **D 7sus4**   **Gm7**

Latin groove

JACK

He cre - a - ted a fan - ta - sy world____ and he got____ him some great____

Gm7   **F/A**   **B♭**   **C**   **B♭/D**   **E♭**

Screwed-Up People Make Great Art - 16 - 8

33475

re - views__ Su - per - na - tu - ral sto - ries of snow-

men and mer - maids and ma - gic shoes__ But when his cha -

rac - ters get__ what they want__ there is of - ten a rude__ sur - prise__

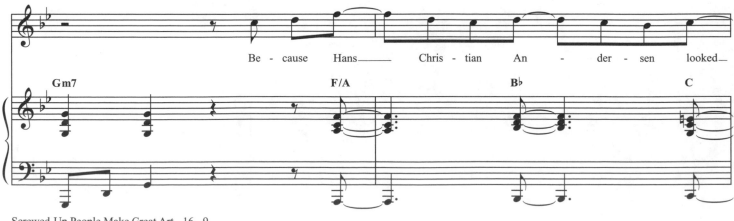

Be - cause Hans__ Chris - tian An - der - sen looked__

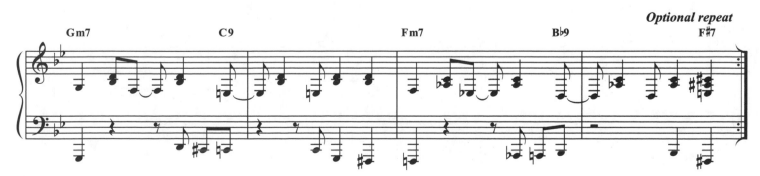

JACK

He ne-ver mar-ried and he ne-ver had kids So his sto-ries were his le-ga-cy

Gm7　　　　C9　　　　Fm7　　　Bb9

Em-peror dude in the nude And a prin-cess who was

F#7　Gm7　　　　C9

kept a-wake all night by a pea_____ On_____ and

Fm7　　　Bb9

Latin groove continues

Screwed-Up People Make Great Art - 16 - 15
33475